THE LIGHT OF THE WORLD

A Book All About Jesus Christ

By Michael J Hnatowicz III

Chapter 1: My Beloved Son

God calls His Son beloved and has given him all things. The Father loves the Son and has Created all things through Him.

He has given Him power and authority over all things. He has made Him a King and Lord over us all.

He is the first begotten of God and first born of all creation. He is the end of all things and all things are renewed through Him.

He was in the beginning with God and is the beginning of all things. He is the end of all things and all things are renewed through Him.

He is the first fruits of the resurrection and life and He is the end of death and sin.

He is the Alpha and Omega who has been given all things by Almighty God the Father. He is the beloved Son of the one and only True God.

God calls his son beloved because He loves His Son and is well pleased with him.

Matthew 3:16 As soon as Jesus was baptized, he went up out of the water. At that moment heaven was opened, and he saw the Spirit of God descending like a dove and alighting on him. 17 and behold, a voice from heaven said, "This is my beloved Son, with whom I am well pleased."

He is the only begotten Son of God and is loved by the Father.

John 5:20 For the Father loves the Son and shows him all he does. Yes, and he will show him even greater works than these, so that you will be amazed.

The Father loves the Son and has given Him all things.

John 3:35 The Father loves the Son and has placed everything in his hands.

He has Created all things through Him and has given Him power and authority over all things.

Colossians 1:16 For in him all things were created: things in heaven and on earth, visible and invisible, whether thrones or powers or rulers or authorities; all things have been created through him and for him. 17 He is before all things, and in him all things hold together.

John 1:3 Through him all things were made; without him nothing was made that has been made.

Matthew 28:18 Then Jesus came to them and said, "All authority in heaven and on earth has been given to me.

He has made Him a King and Lord over us all and has given Him a kingdom.

He is the first begotten of God and first born of all creation.

Colossians 1:18 And he is the head of the body, the church; he is the beginning and the firstborn from among the dead, so that in everything he might have the supremacy.

He was in the beginning with God and is the beginning of all things.

John 1:1-3 In the beginning was the Word and the Word was with God.

He is the end of all things and all things are renewed through him.

2 Corinthians 5:17 Therefore if any man be in Christ, he is a new creature: old things are passed away; behold, all things are become new.

He is the first fruits of the resurrection and life and He is the end of death and sin.

1 Corinthians 5:20 But Christ has indeed been raised from the dead, the first fruits of those who have fallen asleep.

21 For since death came through a man, the resurrection of the dead comes also through a man.

22 For as in Adam all die, so in Christ all will be made alive.

He is the Alpha and Omega who has been given all things by Almighty God the Father.

Revelations 22:13 I am the Alpha and the Omega, the First and the Last, the Beginning and the End.

Revelations 1:8 I am the Alpha and the Omega," says the Lord God, "who is, and who was, and who is to come, the Almighty."

Which of you had he called Son? I am pleased with my Son and I have given my Son all things.

Hebrews 1:5 For to which of the angels did God ever say, "You are my Son; today I have become your Father"? Or again, "I will be his Father, and he will be my Son"?

1:6 And again, when God brings his firstborn into the world, he says, "Let all God's angels worship him."

1:8 But about the Son he says, "Your throne, O God, will last for ever and ever; a scepter of justice will be the scepter of your kingdom.

    The Father loves His Son and gives Him all things. He had put all things under Him and has given Him all power, authority, honor, and glory.

He calls him beloved and has given His only begotten Son for us so that in him we have life. That we glorify him and through him the Father is glorified.

That God did not abandon nor forsake us but saved us through his Son.

That He so loved the world while we were still sinners that He gave His only begotten Son for us so that all who believe shall not perish but have everlasting life.

He has made this Jesus both Lord and Messiah. He is King and Lord over all things and is the anointed Son of God, who the Father is well pleased.

Answersfromthebook.net state that,

There are two instances in the scriptures where the voice of God was heard, expressing His love for His son. When the Lord Jesus was baptized by John the Baptist, the Lord spoke from Heaven.

Matthew 3:16-17 tells us, "And Jesus, when he was baptized, went up straightway out of the water: and, lo, the heavens were opened unto him, and he saw the Spirit of God descending like a dove, and lighting upon him: And lo a voice from heaven, saying, This is my beloved Son, in whom I am well pleased."

Not only was the voice of God heard, but evidence was given of the existence of the Father, the Son, and of the Holy Ghost in this portion, as the Lord Jesus was baptized, the Holy Spirit descended upon Him, and the Father spoke from Heaven, affirming that this Jesus, was indeed, His beloved Son.

When the Lord Jesus was transfigured in the presence of Peter, James, and John, the Lord spoke again from Heaven.

Let us read Matthew 17:1-5, "And after six days Jesus taketh Peter, James, and John his brother, and bringeth them up into a high mountain apart, and was transfigured before them: and his face did shine as the sun, and his raiment was white as the light. And, behold, there appeared unto them Moses and Elias talking with him. Then answered Peter, and said unto Jesus, Lord, it is good for us to be here: if thou wilt, let us make here three tabernacles; one for thee, and one for Moses, and one for Elias. While he yet spoke, behold, a bright cloud overshadowed them: and behold a voice out of the cloud, which said, This is my beloved Son, in whom I am well pleased; hear ye him."

In this portion, the Father not only validates that Jesus was indeed His beloved Son, but He instructs the disciples to listen to Him.

The Old Testament is very instructive; teaching us that God has a Son.

Isaiah 9:6, a very familiar verse tells us, "For unto us a child is born, unto us a son is given: and the government shall be upon his shoulder: and his name shall be called Wonderful, Counsellor, The mighty God, The everlasting Father, The Prince of Peace."

What a precious thought! A child was born, but a son was given. We learn of the eternal son in portions such as

Proverbs 8:22-30, "The LORD possessed me in the beginning of his way, before his works of old. I was set up from everlasting, from the beginning, or ever the earth was. When there were no depths, I was brought forth; when there were no fountains abounding with water. Before the mountains were settled, before the hills was, I brought forth: While as yet he had not made the earth, nor the fields, nor the highest part of the dust of the world. When he prepared the heavens, I was there: when he set a compass upon the face of the depth: When he established the clouds above: when he strengthened the fountains of the deep: When he gave to the sea his decree, that the waters should not pass his commandment: when he appointed the foundations of the earth: Then I was by him, as one brought up with him: and I was daily his delight, rejoicing always before him."

God has an eternal Son, and that son is Jesus.

We have the testimony of many in the New Testament concerning the Lord Jesus being the Son of God. The angel said to the Virgin Mary in Luke 1:35, "...The Holy Ghost shall come upon thee, and the power of the Highest shall overshadow thee: therefore, also that holy thing which shall be born of thee shall be called the Son of God."

John the Baptist said of Jesus in John 1:34, "And I saw, and bare record that this is the Son of God." The disciples said to the Lord in John 6:69, "And we believe and are sure that thou art that Christ, the Son of the living God."

Many of the Jews sought to kill the Lord Jesus because of His claim to be the Son of God as we read in John 19:7 which says, "The Jews answered him, We have a law, and by our law he ought to die, because he made himself the Son of God."

Even demons acknowledged that Jesus is the Son of God as we read in Matthew 8:28-29, "And when he was come to the other side into the country of the Gergesenes, there met him two possessed with devils, coming out of the tombs, exceeding fierce, so that no man might pass by that way. And, behold, they cried out, saying, What have we to do with thee, Jesus, thou Son of God? art thou come hither to torment us before the time?"

We also read of demons acknowledging Jesus as the Son of God in Mark 3:11 which says, "And unclean spirits, when they saw him, fell down before him, and cried, saying, Thou art the Son of God."

At the Lord's crucifixion, we have this testimony in Matthew 27:54, "Now when the centurion, and they that were with him, watching Jesus, saw the earthquake, and those things that were done, they feared greatly, saying, Truly this was the Son of God."

The Father acknowledged Jesus as His very Son, the one in whom He was well pleased.

The Lord Jesus, Himself said in John 8:29, "And he that sent me is with me: The Father hath not left me alone; for I do always those things that please him."

We read in Colossians 1:12-14, "Giving thanks unto the Father, which hath made us meet to be partakers of the inheritance of the saints in light: Who hath delivered us from the power of darkness, and hath translated us into the kingdom of his dear Son: In whom we have *redemption through his blood, even the forgiveness of sins."*

Finally, we have this wonderful testimony of the sonship of Christ in 1 John 5:20, "And we know that the Son of God is come, and hath given us an understanding, that we may know him that is true, and we are in him that is true, even in his Son Jesus Christ. This is the true God, and eternal life."

There are many more scriptures to show us that Jesus Christ is truly the only begotten Son of God

———————————————

Desiring God.org *states, In Matthew 17 Jesus takes Peter, James, and John up on a high mountain. When they are all alone something utterly astonishing happens. All of a sudden God gives Jesus an appearance of glory.*

Verse 2: "His face shone like the sun, and his garments became white as light." Then in verse 5 a bright cloud overshadows them, and God speaks from the cloud, "This is my beloved Son, with whom I am well pleased; listen to him."

First, God gives the disciples a brief glimpse of the true heavenly glory of Jesus. This is what Peter says in 2 Peter 1:17: "[Christ] received honor and glory from God the Father." Then God reveals his heart for the Son and says two things: "I love my son" ("This is my beloved Son"), and "I take pleasure in my Son" ("with whom I am well pleased").

He says this on one other occasion: at Jesus's baptism, as the Holy Spirit comes down and anoints Jesus for his ministry, signifying the Father's love and support — "This is my beloved Son, in whom I am well pleased."

And in the gospel of John, Jesus speaks several times about the Father's love for him: for example, John 3:35, "The Father loves the Son, and has given all things into his hand."

John 5:20: "The Father loves the Son and shows him all that he himself is doing." (See also Matthew 12:18 where Matthew quotes Isaiah 42:1 in reference to Jesus: "Behold, my servant whom I have chosen, my beloved with whom my soul is well pleased." The Hebrew word behind "well pleased" is ratsah, and means "delights in.")

So, our first statement is that God the Father loves the Son, not with any self-denying, sacrificial mercy, but with the love of delight and pleasure. He is well-pleased with his Son. His soul delights in the Son! When he looks at his Son, he enjoys and admires and cherishes and prizes and relishes what he sees.

Answering Islam.org states, The Holy Bible teaches that the Father gave the Son all things:

"All things have been delivered to me by my Father; and no one knows the Son except the Father, and no one knows the Father except the Son and any one to whom the Son chooses to reveal him." Matthew 11:27 "the Father loves the Son and has given all things into his hand." John 3:35 "Jesus, knowing that the Father had given all things into his hands, and that he had come from God and was going to God," John 13:3

Some have deduced from the preceding verses that Jesus is not God since he is receiving all things from someone else, and this other entity must be the one who is God since he has all things to give to whom he wants. After all, God does not receive anything from anyone.

In the first place, it is true that God does not receive anything in the sense that he needs something or depends on his creatures to grant him certain things. Yet this tells us absolutely nothing about the inner relationships that exist within the Godhead.

For instance, the Bible teaches that there are three distinct Persons of Deity who have distinct roles from one another. One Divine Person is the Father, the other is the Son, and the third is the Holy Spirit.

Due to the personal distinctions and unique roles that exist among the Divine Members of the Godhead, it is quite conceivable for one Person of Deity to give certain things or assign specific tasks to the other Divine Persons.

This giving of one Divine Member to another does not violate God being self-sufficient and independent of all needs since God is not receiving anything from anyone outside of himself, outside of his own infinite Being.

Rather, it is the individual Persons within God that are giving to one another.

This leads us to our second and more important point. What the foregoing assumption erroneously overlooks is that the reason why Jesus is said to receive all things is because he is God's Son and therefore the Heir.

The Holy Scriptures teach that the Father created all things through, in, and FOR the Son: "giving thanks to the Father, who has qualified us to share in the inheritance of the saints in light. He has delivered us from the dominion of darkness and transferred us to the kingdom of his beloved Son, in whom we have redemption, the forgiveness of sins. He is the image of the invisible God, the first-born of all creation; for in him all things were created, in heaven and on earth, visible and invisible, whether thrones or dominions or principalities or authorities -- all things were created through him and FOR HIM. HE IS BEFORE ALL THINGS, and IN HIM all things hold together. He is the head of the body, the church; he is the beginning, the first-born from the dead, that in everything he might be pre-eminent." Colossians 1:12-18

Paul teaches in the above passage that Jesus existed before all created things, which means that he is eternal, that all created things were made in, through, and for him since he is God's beloved Son. Paul also states that the Son is actively sustaining all creation, a function which God alone performs.

This explains why Paul calls Christ the Firstborn of all creation, a title which in light of the OT background serves to identify Jesus as the Heir and the One having preeminence over all things:

In conclusion, the Father loves His Son and gives him all things. He has put all things under him and has given him all power, authority, honor, and glory.

He calls him beloved and has given his only begotten Son for us so that in him we have life. That we glorify him and through him the Father is glorified.

That God did not abandon nor forsake us but saved us through his Son. That He so loved the world while we were still sinners that he gave his only begotten Son for us so that all who believe shall not perish but have everlasting life.

He has made this Jesus both Lord and Messiah. He is King and Lord over all things and is the anointed Son of God, the beloved Son of God, who the Father is well pleased.

Chapter 2: King and High Priest

The bloodline of Christ through Mary and Joseph makes Christ King and High Priest through Mary's bloodline and Joseph's. He also is in the order of Melchizedek, where Christ is King and High Priest forever through a heavenly sanctuary.

Through the bloodline of the father, it shows Jesus is the in the line of David through Judah and through his mother's bloodline through Levite.

This puts Christ in line as king and high priest through the tribe of Judah and his father Joseph and through the tribe of Levi through his mother but both being of the house of David.

Jesus is the root of Jesse, the line of David and of the Tribe of Judah. This is the genealogy of Jesus and shows how he is the rightful descendant and heir to the throne.

This is according to his physical life but according to his heavenly reign he reigns as king forever under the order of Melchizedek.

In the order of Melchizedek this is representative of a heavenly sanctuary and a heavenly order. Melchizedek is known as the King of Salem and the high priest.

Genealogies established one's Jewishness, one's tribal identity, one is right to the priesthood and one's right to kingship. Only one line is traced from the beginning to the end of the biblical history, the line of King David. Since the

Messiah was to be of the house of David, this can also be labeled as the messianic line.

As the Seed of the woman, Messiah had to come out of humanity. As the Seed of Abraham, Messiah had to come from the nation of Israel. As the Seed of Judah, he had to be of the tribe of Judah. As the Seed of David, he had to be of the family of David.

In New Testament two genealogies are found in Matthew and in Luke. Matthew focuses on the Patriarchal Line of Jesus birth through Joseph, while Luke focuses on the Matriarchal line though Mary. Through Joseph, Jesus, had the Royal line of David and right to the throne. Joseph being from tribe of Judah and House of David.

Mary was the real line of Jesus from him being born from a woman and Joseph was his adopted father. Mary was also of the House of David; her Father was Heli.

So, like Joseph, Mary was a member of the house of David. But unlike Joseph, she came from David's son, Nathan, not Solomon.

Mary was a member of the house of David apart from Jeconiah. (Jeconiah curse) Since Jesus was Mary's son, he too was a member of the house of David, apart from Jeconiah.

Since he was to have no human father, his nationality and his tribal identity would come entirely from his mother. True, this is contrary to the norm, but so is a virgin birth. With the Messiah, things would be different.

Mary's Father Heli (tribe of Judah) married a woman from the (tribe of Levi) making Jesus' half from the tribe of

Judah (King lineage) and half tribe of Levi (Priest lineage) this is how He rightfully is called King of Kings and Lord of Lords.

His birth and lineage from mother n father traces back to House of David and puts Him rightfully as King and High Priest.

Desiring God.org writes, "Why, when you compare Matthew's genealogy with Luke's between David and Jesus, are they almost completely different?

All the names but two are different. A major commentary published in 1978 by I. H. Marshall says, "It is only right therefore to admit that the problem caused by the existence of the two genealogies is insoluble with the evidence presently at our disposal" (p. 159).

What he means is not that the two are in unresolvable conflict. There are suggested solutions, but we just do not know enough to be sure these solutions are the proper ones.

I will just mention two. One suggestion is that, from David to Jesus, Matthew "gives the legal descendants of David— the men who would have been legally the heir to the Davidic throne if that throne had continued—while Luke gives the descendants of David in that particular time to which finally Joseph, the husband of Mary, belonged" (Machen, Virgin Birth, p. 204).

So, for example, Luke says in 3:31 that the son of David was Nathan (2 Samuel 5:14), while Matthew in 1:6 says the son of David was Solomon, who was heir to the throne. The two lines could easily merge whenever one of Nathan's descendants became the rightful heir to the throne.

The other suggested solution is that Luke gives Mary's genealogy and Matthew gives Joseph's as Jesus' legal father.

The key to this interpretation is extending the parenthesis of verse 23 to include Joseph. So, it would read, "Jesus was about 30 years old, being the son (as was supposed of Joseph) of Heli etc."

By including "of Joseph" in the parenthesis the point is made that Jesus is really the son of Mary, not Joseph, and Heli is his grandfather (Mary's father).

Both of these solutions are possible; the first is more probable; but neither can be proved.

The lineage of Jesus is traced back through his mother's lineage and the father's lineage. Matthew and Luke both trace Jesus back to the root of Jesse, the root of David, and the son of Adam. Through both his mother and father he is of the house of David with both being of the tribe of Judah and Levi. This makes Jesus the heir to David which makes him king and through Levitical order makes him high priest. Not only through this earthly order is Christ King and High Priest but also through the order of Melchizedek.

In the order of Melchizedek Christ becomes King and High Priest forever. Melchizedek in the Bible is known as prominent figure in which he has no origin or beginning and is highly regarded as King of Salem and High Priest through a heavenly order.

Watv.org states In the Bible there are two divisions orders of priesthood: the order of Aaron and the order of Melchizedek.

1. The order of Aaron

The order of Aaron is a priestly division in which the priests conducted sacrifices according to the laws and regulations of the old covenant. Aaron was a Levite, so the order of Aaron is also called the Levitical priesthood [the order of Levites].

Abraham was the father of Isaac, Isaac the father of Jacob, Jacob the father of 12 sons including Levi, who was the third son of Jacob and his wife Leah. Jacob and his family moved to Egypt when his son Joseph became a ruler of Egypt, and they left Egypt after 430 years. Millions of Jacob's descendants headed to Canaan, following their leader, Moses.

After crossing the Red Sea, the Israelites entered the desert, and when Moses received the Ten Commandments on Mount Sinai, they built the tabernacle to keep the Ten Commandments in. At that time, Aaron the older brother of Moses was the high priest whose main duty was to offer sacrifices to God in the tabernacle, and the entire tribe of Levi, which Moses and Aron belonged to, was called to serve in the temple.

When the Levitical priests offered sacrifices to God for the people's sins, they slaughtered a lamb or goat. Over a period of 1,500 years from the time of Aaron until the time when Jesus established the new covenant, all the descendants of Levi [the tribe of Levi] continued to serve as priests according to the order of Aaron in the earthly sanctuary.

2. The order of Melchizedek

Besides the order of Aaron, there are also references to the "order of Melchizedek" in the Bible; Christ is described as the "High Priest in the order of Melchizedek." It enters the inner sanctuary behind the curtain, where Jesus, who went before us, has entered on our behalf. He has become a high priest forever, in the order of Melchizedek. Heb 6:19-20

So, let us study Melchizedek first.

Melchizedek was a person who lived during the time of Abraham about 2,000 years before Jesus came to this earth. He represents Christ. Melchizedek is mentioned in only two places in the Old Testament; he is just described as "king of Salem" who lived in the time of Abraham. There are no exact records of how he became a priest or where "Salem" was located.

This mysterious figure, Melchizedek, brought out bread and wine to bless Abraham as he was returning from a battle where he had defeated the kings and their armies to rescue his nephew Lot. The Bible calls this Melchizedek "priest of God Most High."

After Abram returned from defeating Kedorlaomer and the kings allied with him . . . Then Melchizedek king of Salem brought out bread and wine. He was priest of God Most

High, and he blessed Abram, saying, "Blessed be Abram by God Most High, Creator of heaven and earth. And blessed be God Most High, who delivered your enemies into your hand." Then Abram gave him a tenth of everything.
Genesis 14:17-20

In the time of Abraham, animal sacrifices were offered to God according to the tradition of Abel's sacrifice. However, Melchizedek offered a sacrifice of bread and wine to God. The Apostle Paul explained a lot about Melchizedek. He described Melchizedek as "king of righteousness" and "king of peace," saying that like the Son of God he remains a priest forever.

He also wrote in detail that the Levites and even Levi himself the father of the tribe of Levi, who would collect a tenth from each of the twelve tribes of Israel, paid the tenth to Melchizedek through Abraham, and that Christ became a priest in the order of Melchizedek with an oath from God, while others in the earthly sanctuary became priests without any oath (Heb 7:1-28).

3. Christ who followed the order of Melchizedek
About 1,100 years before Jesus came to this earth, David, being moved by the Holy Spirit, prophesied that the Lord [Christ] would come to serve as a High Priest in the order of Melchizedek.

The LORD says to my Lord: "Sit at my right hand until I make your enemies a footstool for your feet." The LORD will extend your mighty scepter from Zion . . . The LORD has sworn and will not change his mind: "You are a priest forever, in the order of Melchizedek."
Psalms 110:1-4

Jesus interpreted the "Lord" whom David mentioned in the book of Psalms as "Christ."

While the Pharisees were gathered together, Jesus asked them, "What do you think about the Christ? Whose son, is he?" "The son of David," they replied. He said to them, "How is it then that David, speaking by the Spirit, calls him 'Lord'? For he says, "'The Lord said to my Lord: "Sit at my right hand until I put your enemies under your feet."' If then David calls him 'Lord,' how can he be his son?" Matthew 22:41-45

David prophesied that Christ would be a High Priest in the order of Melchizedek, and the LORD God [Jehovah] promised with an oath that He would surely fulfill it.

Just as Melchizedek blessed Abraham through bread and wine, Jesus blessed human beings through bread and wine at the Passover.

So, the disciples did as Jesus had directed them and prepared the Passover . . . While they were eating, Jesus took bread, gave thanks and broke it, and gave it to his disciples, saying, "Take and eat; this is my body." Then he took the cup [wine] "Drink from it, all of you. This is my blood of the covenant, which is poured out for many for the forgiveness of sins." Matthew 26:17-28

Why did God raise another priest from a different order— the order of Melchizedek—instead of the order of Aaron, which had been handed down over a period of 1,500 years?

As aforementioned, the sacrifices offered according to the order of Aaron were a copy and shadow of what Christ *would establish later; for the order of Aaron [the Levitical priesthood] could not forgive sins.*

If perfection could have been attained through the Levitical priesthood . . . why was there still need for another priest to come—one in the order of Melchizedek, not in the order of Aaron? Hebrews 7:11

The tithe Abraham gave Melchizedek represents our offering to Christ who has come as the High Priest in the order of Melchizedek. Just as Abraham gave Melchizedek a tenth of everything when Melchizedek gave him a blessing with bread and wine, God's people in Christ give a tenth to Christ because He has given us the blessing of eternal life with the bread and wine of the Passover as the High Priest in the order of Melchizedek.

    In conclusion, not only does Christ receive Kingship through the line of David and the earthly throne but received the heavenly throne through the order of Melchizedek.

Not only does he become High Priest through the earthly sanctuary and through the order of Aaron but becomes High Priest forever through the order of Melchizedek.

So, in heaven and on earth Christ reigns as King and Lord forever and gives the offering of bread and wine or his body and blood as a continuous perpetual sacrifice once and for all which makes him High Priest forever.

Chapter 3: Power Authority Honor and Glory

Christ has received all power, authority, honor, and glory from God. He has appointed and anointed him as King and Lord.

All power and authority have been given to Christ. He is over all creation and he is head over man. We are subject to Christ our King and he is subjected to God our Father.

For all things have been put under him but not including God himself. Christ is the head of man and God is the head of Christ.

All power and authority have been given to him by the Father so that Christ is glorified and in him the father is glorified.

A king has sovereignty and power and authority over the land and its people. Christ is king of kings because he has sovereign power from God and a kingdom.

_____

Christ has received all power authority honor and glory from God the Father.

Matthew 28:18 Then Jesus came to them and said, "All authority in heaven and on earth has been given to me.

2 Peter 1:17 He received honor and glory from God the Father when the voice came to him from the Majestic Glory, saying, "This is my Son, whom I love; with him I am well pleased."

God has appointed and anointed him as Lord and Messiah.

Hebrews 1:2 but in these last days he has spoken to us by his Son, whom he appointed heir of all things, and through whom also he made the universe.

Ephesians 1:22 And God placed all things under his feet and appointed him to be head over everything for the church,

Hebrews 2:5 You made him a little lower than the angels; you crowned him with glory and honor and put everything under his feet." In putting everything under him, God left nothing that is not subject to him.

Acts 2:36 "Therefore let all Israel be assured of this: God has made this Jesus, whom you crucified, both Lord and Messiah."

All power and authority has been given to Christ. He is Lord over all creation and the head of man.

John 3:35 The Father loves the Son and has placed everything in his hands.

Colossians 1:18 And he is the head of the body, the church; he is the beginning and the firstborn from among the dead, so that in everything he might have the supremacy.

1 Corinthians 11:13 But I want you to realize that the head of every man is Christ, and the head of the woman is man, and the head of Christ is God.

We are subject to Christ our King and he is subjected to God our Father. For all things have been put under him but not including God himself. Christ is the head of man and God is the head of Christ.

1 Corinthians 15:24 Then the end will come, when he hands over the kingdom to God the Father after he has destroyed all dominion, authority, and power. 25 For he must reign until he has put all his enemies under his feet. 26 The last enemy to be destroyed is death. 27 For he "has put everything under his feet." Now when it says that "everything" has been put under him, it is clear that this does not include God himself, who put everything under Christ. 28 When he has done this, then the Son himself will be made subject to him who put everything under him, so that God may be all in all.

All power and authority has been given to him by the Father so that Christ is glorified and in him the father is glorified.

John 13:31 As soon as Judas left the room, Jesus said, "The time has come for the Son of Man to enter into his glory, and God will be glorified because of him.

John 13:32 And since God receives glory because of the Son, he will give his own glory to the Son, and he will do so at once.

Christ glory is that he is the Son of God who did the will of God and who glorifies the Father.

In doing so he had received power and authority, supremacy, and Lordship, over all things in heaven and on earth. This makes him the King of Kings who received a kingdom and his people by God.

Hebrews 1: 8 But about the Son he says, "Your throne, O God, will last for ever and ever; a scepter of justice will be the scepter of your kingdom.

9 You have loved righteousness and hated wickedness; therefore God, your God, has set you above your companions by anointing you with the oil of joy."

John 10:27 My sheep listen to my voice; I know them, and they follow me. 28 I give them eternal life, and they shall never perish; no one will snatch them out of my hand. 29 My Father, who has given them to me, is greater than all; no one can snatch them out of my Father's hand.

Theology of work.org writes, "In yesterday's reflection, we focused on the glorious sovereignty of Jesus Christ, whom God the father has enthroned "far above all rule and authority, power and dominion, and every name that is invoked, not only in the present age but also in the one to come" (1:21).

In verse 22, Paul elaborates further on the authority of Christ, "And God placed all things under his feet and appointed him to be head over everything for the church."

If we read this verse quickly, we might miss its distinctive picture of the headship of Christ. Ordinarily, we speak of Christ as the head of the church. Indeed, this language will be found later in Ephesians (5:23).

But, in 1:22, Paul says something different. Translating very precisely, this verse reads, "[God] gave him [Christ] as *head over all things for the church [or through the church]." Here, the point is not Christ's headship of the church, but rather his headship over all things for the church. How are we to understand this verse and its relevance to us?*

The word "head" (kephale in Greek) can mean "authority" or "source," in addition to "head" as a body part. In our passage, Paul is clearly using kephale in the sense of authority. He has just said that God the Father has enthroned Christ above everything else in all creation.

Expanding on this, Paul uses body imagery to illustrate the superior authority of Christ. All things are under his feet, and he is the head over all things.

When we look at our world, it may be hard to envision Christ as head over everything. We are surrounded by so much brokenness, unrighteousness, and injustice. We might wonder: If Christ is head over everything, why is everything so messed up?

The quick biblical answer is that things are such a mess because of human sin. But God is in the process of making everything right through Christ. As we saw earlier in Ephesians, in the future, God will "bring unity to all things in heaven and on earth under Christ" (1:10).

Christianity.com writes, "In Revelation 1:5 we also see the metaphorical sense of the term, showing Jesus' supremacy in authority and kingship after his resurrection.

Biblical scholar G.K. Beale explains,

John views Jesus as the ideal Davidic king on an escalated eschatological level, whose death and resurrection have resulted in his eternal kingship and in the kingship of his beloved children.

"Firstborn" refers to the high, privileged position that Christ has as a result of the resurrection from the dead. Christ has gained such a sovereign position over the cosmos, not in the sense that he is recognized as the first-created being of all creation or as the origin of creation, but in the sense that he is the inaugurator of the new creation by means of his resurrection.

We can draw all this together to see that there are two central ideas in the title "firstborn of the dead" in Revelation 1:5.

First, the allusion to Psalm 89 shows that Jesus fulfills all history as the messianic King descended from the line of David.

Second, being the "firstborn of the dead" means that Jesus is both the first to rise and the first in supremacy. He is the first to rise from the dead and thus the first of the new creation.

He is also the inaugurator of the new creation and sovereign over everything. He is the rightful heir to it all.

In conclusion, Christ has received all power, authority, honor, and glory from the Father, Almighty God. That He is the Son of God who is seated at the right hand of God.

Christ is Almighty who has been given all power and authority. True God from True God. This is what makes Christ Lord and King being put above all things and all things being made subject to him.

He is Christ and Messiah being the savior and anointed one appointed by God. He was before all things and is after all things.

He was made first and is the last and all things renewed through him so that he is made supreme in all things. His glory is that He is the Son of God and in him He glorifies the Father.

He is the Son of God who has inherited the Kingdom of God and who is Lord and King holding all power and authority in heaven and on earth and has received honor and glory as the Lamb of God, the one and only Son of God.

Chapter 4: Lord of Lords

Christ is Lord over all creation given power and authority by Almighty God the Father. He has made Christ both Lord and Messiah.

He is king and lord and has supreme authority. God has given him this kingdom and made him a king.

Christ says my kingdom is not of this world. His Kingdom is of Heaven. He is Lord over all the earth and heaven. He is called the King of Kings and Lord of lords.

Jesus Christ is Lord. He is Lord over all creation having supreme power and authority over all.

He is Lord of Lords and King of Kings. He has a kingdom, and his kingdom will have no end.

What is a Lord? A Lord is a King or ruler having supreme authority over a land and its people. There are many kings of many nations who rule over their land. These are the kings of the earth. Christ is King and Lord over all the kings of the earth.

A king or lord represents a position of the highest authority. Just as a king is over the land, Jesus is King over all the earth and all kings of every nation.

This is why He is the King of Kings and Lord of Lords. For there are many Lords in the earth but Jesus Christ is the Lord of all Lords.

He sits above the earth and the earth is his footstool. His Kingdom is not of this world but is the Kingdom of Heaven.

He is ruler, king, and lord over the heaven and the earth. He has been appointed and anointed as the Son of God the Messiah and King and Lord over all creation.

He is above all power authority and dominion. He has been given Power Honor and Glory and was exalted to the highest position sitting at the right hand of God.

God has given him his people and those who are His. God has given him all power and authority and made this Jesus both Lord and Messiah.

That every tongue will confess, and every knee bow that Jesus Christ is Lord, to the Glory of the Father.

In the end, his kingdom will come down from heaven on the earth and he will rule as King and Lord forever. This is also known as the millennial kingdom and in the end paradise on earth.

Jesus Christ is Lord. He is Lord over all creation having supreme power and authority over all.

Matthew 28:17 When they saw Him, they worshiped Him; but some were doubtful.

18 And Jesus came up and spoke to them, saying, "All authority has been given to Me in heaven and on earth.

He is Lord of Lords and King of Kings. He has a kingdom and his kingdom will have no end.

1 Timothy 6:15 which He will bring about at the proper time—He who is the blessed and only Sovereign, the King of kings and Lord of lords,

Ephesians 1:21 far above all rule and authority and power and dominion, and every name that is named, not only in this age but also in the one to come.

There are many kings of many nations who rule over their land. These are the kings of the earth. Christ is King and Lord over all the kings of the earth.

Revelations 1:4-5 Grace to you and peace, from Him who is and who was and who is to come, and from the seven Spirits who are before His throne, and from Jesus Christ, the faithful witness, the firstborn of the dead, and the ruler of the kings of the earth.

A king or Lord represents a position of the highest authority. Just as a king is over the land, Jesus is King over all the earth and all kings of every nation.

Matthew 11:27 All things have been handed over to Me by My Father;

Philippians 2:9 For this reason also, God highly exalted Him, and bestowed on Him the name which is above every name,

Colossians 2:10 and in Him you have been made complete, and He is the head over all rule and authority;

This is why He is the King of Kings and Lord of Lords. For there are many Lords in the earth but Jesus Christ is the Lord of all Lords.

Revelations 17:14 These will wage war against the Lamb, and the Lamb will overcome them, because He is Lord of lords and King of kings, and those who are with Him are the called and chosen and faithful."

Revelations 19:16 And on His robe and on His thigh He has a name written, "KING OF KINGS, AND LORD OF LORDS."

He sits above the earth and the earth is his footstool.

Psalm 8:6 You make him to rule over the works of Your hands;
You have put all things under his feet,

Psalm 110:1 A Psalm of David.
The Lord says to my Lord:
"Sit at My right hand
Until I make Your enemies a footstool for Your feet."

His Kingdom is not of this world but is the Kingdom of Heaven.

Psalms 103:19 The LORD has established his throne in heaven, and his kingdom rules over all.

Ephesians 1:20 which He brought about in Christ, when He raised Him from the dead and seated Him at His right hand in the heavenly places,

He is ruler, king, and lord over the heaven and the earth.

1 Peter 3:22 who is at the right hand of God, having gone into heaven, after angels and authorities and powers had been subjected to Him.

John 3:35 The Father loves the Son and has given all things into His hand.

John 17:2 even as You gave Him authority over all flesh, that to all whom You have given Him, He may give eternal life.

He has been appointed and anointed as the Son of God the Messiah and King and Lord over all creation.

John 19:11 Jesus answered, "You would have no authority over Me, unless it had been given you from above;

John 3:31 "He who comes from above is above all, he who is of the earth is from the earth and speaks of the earth. He who comes from heaven is above all.

He is above all power authority and dominion. He has been given Power Honor and Glory and was exalted to the highest position sitting at the right hand of God.

Acts 2:34 For it was not David who ascended into heaven, but he himself says:
'The Lord said to my Lord,
"Sit at My right hand,

God has given him his people and those who are His. God has given him all power and authority and made this Jesus both Lord and Messiah.

John 10:27 My sheep listen to my voice; I know them, and they follow me. 28 I give them eternal life, and they shall never perish; no one will snatch them out of my hand. 29 My Father, who has given them to me, is greater than all; no one can snatch them out of my Father's hand.

Acts 2:36 Therefore let all the house of Israel know for certain that God has made Him both Lord and Christ—this Jesus whom you crucified."

That every tongue will confess, and every knee bow that Jesus Christ is Lord, to the Glory of the Father.

Philippians 2:11 and every tongue confess that Jesus Christ is Lord, to the glory of God the Father.

Philippians 2:10 so that at the name of Jesus every knee will bow, of those who are in heaven and on earth and under the earth,

In the end, his kingdom will come down from heaven on the earth and he will rule as King and Lord forever.

1 Corinthians 15:24 then comes the end, when He hands over the kingdom to the God and Father, when He has abolished all rule and all authority and power.

1 Corinthians 8:6 yet for us there is but one God, the Father, from whom are all things and we exist for Him; and one Lord, Jesus Christ, by whom are all things, and we exist through Him.

1 Timothy 1:2 To Timothy, my true child in the faith: Grace, mercy and peace from God the Father and Christ Jesus our Lord.

2 Peter 1:2 Grace and peace be multiplied to you in the knowledge of God and of Jesus our Lord;

2 Peter 1:11 for in this way the entrance into the eternal kingdom of our Lord and Savior Jesus Christ will be abundantly supplied to you.

This is also known as the millennial kingdom and in the end paradise on earth.

Revelations 20:6 Blessed and holy are those who share in the first resurrection. The second death has no power over them, but they will be priests of God and of Christ and will reign with him for a thousand years.

Zechariah 14:9 And the LORD will be king over all the earth. On that day there will be one LORD—his name alone will be worshiped.

Revelations 21:2 I saw the Holy City, the new Jerusalem, coming down out of heaven from God, prepared as a bride beautifully dressed for her husband.

Matthew 6:10 your kingdom come, your will be done, on earth as it is in heaven.

Christianity.Com quotes, "In the New Testament, Lord is the most frequently used title for Jesus Christ. Although we rarely use this term in our daily lives, we are all quite familiar with another word: boss.

That is basically what Lord means—one possessing authority, power, and control. The Word of God describes Jesus as the head of the church, the ruler over all creation, and the Lord of lords and King of kings (Col. 1:15-18; Rev. 3:14, 17:14).

Jesus is Lord: Scripture Meaning

Following the resurrection, the term "Lord," being applied to Jesus, became more than an indication of devotion or respect. Stating, "Jesus is Lord," became a way of recognizing Jesus' divine standing.

References of Jesus as Lord started with Thomas' declaration when Jesus arrived at the apostles after His resurrection: "Thomas said to him, 'My Lord and my God!'" (John 20:28).

From thereafter, the message of the Apostles was that Jesus is Lord, signifying that "Jesus is God."

Peter's sermon on the Day of Pentecost carried that idea: "Let all Israel be assured of this: God has made this Jesus, whom you crucified, both Lord and Messiah" (Acts 2:36).

Peter later declared this in the house of Cornelius, stating that Jesus is "Lord of all" (Acts 10:36).

It is important to note that in Romans 10:9 Jesus' lordship is connected to His resurrection: "If you declare with your mouth, 'Jesus is Lord,' and believe in your heart that God raised him from the dead, you will be saved."

The declaration "Jesus is Lord" indicates that Jesus is God. Jesus holds "all authority in heaven and on earth" (Matthew 28:18). He is "Lord of the Sabbath" (Luke 6:5); "our only Sovereign and Lord" (Jude 1:4); and "the Lord of lords" (Revelation 17:14).

What Makes Jesus a "Lord"?

The realm of Christ's reign covers everything that happens in heaven and on the earth. No one—not even those who deny His existence—can be free of His rule or outside His sphere of authority. Although Satan tries to convince us that liberty is found in doing what we want, true freedom is acquired only through submission to Christ's loving lordship.

Even death cannot release anyone from the authority of God's Son. He is Lord of both the living and the dead. All people must decide to either yield or rebel against Him, but they have the opportunity to make this choice only while they are still living. After death, they will acknowledge Christ's lordship through accountability to Him. If we have not bowed the knee to Jesus in life, we will be forced to bend it in the judgment.

Have you submitted to Christ's rule over your life? His authority causes anger or fear in individuals who have not yet yielded to Him, but those who have experienced His loving kindness trusted in His goodness and surrendered to His authority take comfort in knowing Him as the Lord of their lives.

Taken from "Lord of the Living and the Dead" from In Touch Ministries (used by permission).

The 1000 Year Millennium Kingdom
By: Michael Bradley

Now that Jesus has returned back to our earth for the second and final time – what exactly is He going to do?

He is going to be setting up a 1000-year Millennium Kingdom in which He will literally rule this entire earth from the city of Jerusalem in Israel. Here is what the Bible has to say about what will be going on during this time period.

The Bible says this period will be a time of perfect peace. Jesus will rule this entire earth from the city of Jerusalem, and He, and He alone will be the only official Ruler and King of this earth. Men will no longer war with one another and even the wild beasts like tigers and lions will be tame.

All of the saints who have been living with Jesus in heaven will be coming down with Him to help Him rule the nations of this world. Jesus will be the only God people will worship and serve.

All other false religions will have been completely done away with. People will live long lives, possibly up to 1000 years like they did before the flood of Noah.

Here are the main verses from Scripture that will give us this specific information.

Jesus Will Rule This Earth from the City of Jerusalem

Some people think that Jesus will not be literally ruling this earth from the city of Jerusalem. They think He will be ruling from Heaven where He is at now. I believe this view is wrong.

The following Scripture verses will tell us, without any other possible interpretation, that Jesus will literally be ruling this entire earth from the city of Jerusalem, not from Heaven where He is at right now.

1. This first verse is from the Book of Psalms. It is God the Father making a statement that He will set His Son Jesus on the holy hill of Zion where He will literally rule from. God is saying that He is going to give Jesus the entire earth as His possession.

2. This next verse says that God the Father will be giving Jesus the throne of King David, which is from Jerusalem, and that His kingdom will last forever.

3. This next verse tells us that this kingdom will never be destroyed and that it will not be left to humans to try and manage. Humans have made nothing but a mess of things over the course of human history, and God will no longer be putting up with us trying to run the world. This verse tells us that Jesus' kingdom will now consume all of the other earthly kingdoms of this earth and break them into pieces.

4. This next verse tells us that all peoples, nations, and languages will serve Jesus. Jesus, and Jesus alone, will be our earthly King, and no one else will be worshiped as a god or king. Jesus will be the sole supreme Ruler and King of this earth forever and ever!

5. This next verse tells us that our earthly government will be on Jesus' shoulders. It says we will have a peace on this earth that will have no end!
This verse also reaffirms that Jesus will be upon the throne of David and that He will rule with justice and righteousness from His throne. He will be called the Prince of Peace! We will literally have heaven on earth with Jesus in complete control of everything.

6. This next verse tells us that Jesus will literally be dwelling in the midst of Jerusalem. It says that Jerusalem will be called the holy mountain of God. I believe this verse is telling us that Jesus will literally rule this earth from the city of Jerusalem – not heaven!

7. Here is another good verse that will tell us that Jesus will literally be dwelling in our midst. When the Bible says that Jesus will be dwelling in our midst, I believe this is literal interpretation – that He will literally, not symbolically or figuratively, but literally be dwelling and living among us in this Millennium Kingdom.

The New Heaven and New Earth
By: Michael Bradley
Bible-knowledge.com

Now that Satan, all of his fallen angels, and all of unsaved humanity have been cast into the Lake of Fire and

Brimstone, there is now only one thing left. God will now be giving the rest of saved humanity their final reward – the New Heaven and New Earth.

Believe it or not, this is actually going to be better than what we will get during the Millennium Kingdom. This will be our final abode and resting place with the Lord and something very awesome happens when we get this New Heaven and New Earth.

When we receive the 1000-year Millennium Kingdom, we get Jesus Himself literally coming down from heaven to rule our earth from the city of Jerusalem in Israel.

When we get the New Heaven and New Earth – we will now get God the Father Himself literally coming down from heaven to our New Earth to live and dwell with all of us forever and ever!

In other words, we will now have both God and Jesus living with all of us forever and ever in this New Heaven and New Earth!

    In conclusion, Christ is Lord of Lords and King of Kings. He is the head of man and all creation and the head of Christ is God.

He has been given all power and authority and has been made a King. He is above all the kings of the earth and is the Lord of all lords. He is supreme on the earth and is the Sovereign Lord who is above all things.

A Lord is a ruler or king who has supreme power and authority over the land and its people. Christ is the King of kings who has been given all power and authority and a kingdom in which he will rule.

He has been given power to forgive sins for in him is the forgiveness of sins. He has been exalted to the highest position and seated at God's right hand. There is the throne of God and of the Lamb for he reigns with God forever.

That Christ will return and rule on the earth from Jerusalem. In the end, he gives all power and authority back to God and is the Lamb of God and the Light of the World who takes away the sins of the world and defeats the powers of darkness.

Then New Jerusalem will come down from heaven on the earth and God will be with men and the kingdom will come. As in the Our Father prayer, His Kingdom come, and His will be done on earth as it is in heaven.

Chapter 5: Alpha and Omega

He is the first and the last. The beginning and the end. He is the first born of all creation and the end of all things. He is the first fruits being the first resurrected of the dead.

All things are made new in him. He is the Word who was in the beginning with God and the Lamb who is in the end.

He is the beginning of all things and the end of all things. He is in Genesis in the beginning and is in the end in Revelations. He is the Alpha and the Omega.

He is the first and the last. The beginning and the end.

Revelations 22:13 "I am Alpha and Omega, the beginning and the end, the first and the last."

He is the first born of all creation and the end of all things. All things are renewed through him and he is the first fruits of the resurrection.

Colossians 1:15 The Son is the image of the invisible God, the firstborn over all creation. 16 For in him all things were created: things in heaven and on earth, visible and invisible, whether thrones or powers or rulers or authorities; all things have been created through him and for him. 17 He is before all things, and in him all things hold together. 18 And he is the head of the body, the church; he is the beginning and the firstborn from among the dead, so that in everything he might have the supremacy.

Corinthians 15:22 For as in Adam all die, so in Christ all will be made alive. 23 But each in turn: Christ, the first fruits; then, when he comes, those who belong to him.

Another translation from NLV is, "But there is an order to this resurrection: Christ was raised as the first of the harvest; then all who belong to Christ will be raised when he comes back.

Grace Bible Ny. Org writes, "Verse 20 is simply a statement of the reality of the resurrection of Jesus Christ from the dead. Paul has already proven that to be true by citing the many eyewitnesses of that fact. Paul also points out here that Jesus is the "first fruits of those who are asleep," a euphemism for those who have died. "First fruits" is a double reference indicating not only that Jesus was the first to be resurrected of many who will be resurrected in the future, but it is also a reference to the Old Testament requirement that the first of any harvested crops were to be brought to the Lord as an offering. Jesus was in fact that offering.

He is the word who was in the beginning and the lamb who is in the end. He is the beginning of all things and the end of all things. He is in Genesis in the beginning and is in the end in revelations.

John 1:1 In the beginning was the Word, and the Word was with God, and the Word was God. 2 He was with God in the beginning. 3 Through him all things were made; without him nothing was made that has been made.

Genesis 1:1 In the beginning God created the heavens and the earth. 2 Now the earth was formless and empty, darkness was over the surface of the deep, and the Spirit of God was hovering over the waters. 3 And God said, "Let there be light," and there was light. 4 God saw that the light was good,

Revelations 5:12 In a loud voice they were saying: "Worthy is the Lamb, who was slain, to receive power and wealth and wisdom and strength and honor and glory and praise!" 13 Then I heard every creature in heaven and on earth and under the earth and on the sea, and all that is in them, saying: "To him who sits on the throne and to the Lamb be praise and honor and glory and power, for ever and ever!"

Got questions.org writes, "Jesus proclaimed Himself to be the "Alpha and Omega" in Revelation 1:8; 21:6; and 22:13. Alpha and omega are the first and last letters of the Greek alphabet. Among the Jewish rabbis, it was common to use the first and the last letters of the Hebrew alphabet to denote the whole of anything, from beginning to end. Jesus as the beginning and end of all things is a reference to no one but the true God. This statement of eternity could apply only to God. It is seen especially in Revelation 22:13, where Jesus proclaims that He is "the Alpha and the Omega, the First and the Last, the Beginning and the End."

One of the meanings of Jesus being the "Alpha and Omega" is that He was at the beginning of all things and will be at the close. It is equivalent to saying He always existed and always will exist. It was Christ, as second Person of the Trinity, who brought about the creation: "Through him all things were made; without him nothing was made that has been made" (John 1:3), and His Second Coming will be the beginning of the end of creation as we know it (2 Peter 3:10). As God incarnate, He has no beginning, nor will He have any end with respect to time, being from everlasting to everlasting.

A second meaning of Jesus as the "Alpha and Omega" is that the phrase identifies Him as the God of the Old Testament. Isaiah ascribes this aspect of Jesus' nature as part of the triune God in several places. "I, the Lord, am the first, and with the last I am He" (41:4). "I am the first, and I am the last; and beside me there is no God" (Isaiah 44:6). "I am he; I am the first, I also am the last" (Isaiah 48:12). These are clear indications of the eternal nature of the Godhead.

Christ, as the Alpha and Omega, is the first and last in so many ways. He is the "author and finisher" of our faith (Hebrews 12:2), signifying that He begins it and carries it through to completion. He is the totality, the sum and substance of the Scriptures, both of the Law and of the Gospel (John 1:1, 14). He is the fulfilling end of the Law (Matthew 5:17), and He is the beginning subject matter of the gospel of grace through faith, not of works (Ephesians 2:8-9). He is found in the first verse of Genesis and in the last verse of Revelation. He is the first and last, the all in all *of salvation, from the justification before God to the final sanctification of His people.*

Christianity.com writes Revelation 1:8 supports God's sovereignty with three statements, the first of which expresses the eternity of God: "'I am the Alpha and the Omega,' says the Lord God." God reigns over all since he is before and after all things.

This should be understood as Jesus is the Alpha and Omega, says the Lord God. Christ reigns over all since he is before and after all things.

───────────────

    In Conclusion, God the Father has no beginning or no end. He is before the beginning and after the end. God is eternal and self-existent.

The Word of God was in the beginning with God and is the only begotten of the Father. He is the beginning of all things and the first born of all creation.

All things were made through him by him and for him. He is the end of all creation and all things are made new in Him.

Christ is the beginning and the end, the first and the last, the Alpha and Omega. He is co-eternal and co-existent with the Father being begotten of God.

He was in the beginning with God and reigns with God forever as the Word of God, Son of God, and Lamb of God, who was who is and who is to come again.

Chapter 6

Who was who is and who is to come

Jesus is the Word of God, Son of God, and Lamb of God.

Who was in the beginning with God who is the only begotten Son of God and the Lamb of God who is the one to come again.

The Word was in the beginning with God the Son is the only begotten of the Father and the lamb of God died for the sins of the world and will come again.

The Word of God who was in the beginning with God. The Word who became flesh. Jesus Christ is the Word of God.

He was before Moses He was before Abraham. He was in the beginning with God. He is the living Word of God.

Jesus is the Word of God, Son of God, and Lamb of God. Who was who is and who is to come.

    The Word of God who was in the beginning with God. The Word who was in heaven with God in the beginning. The Word who came down from heaven and was made flesh.

John 1:1 In the beginning was the Word, and the Word was with God, and the Word was God. The same was in the beginning with God.

1 John 5:7 For there are three that bear record in heaven, the Father, the Word, and the Holy Ghost: and these three are one.

John 1:14 The Word became flesh and made his dwelling among us. We have seen his glory, the glory of the one and only Son, who came from the Father, full of grace and truth.

John 17:5 And now, Father, glorify me in your presence with the glory I had with you before the world began.

As Jesus was in Heaven in the beginning before all things He is known as the Word of God who proceeds and is begotten of God. This Word became flesh which is Jesus coming down from heaven and being born a man. This is where he is called the Son of God.

The Son of God who was born man and born of God. The Son of Man and the Son of God. The Word of God who became flesh. Who came down from heaven and was sent by God to be light and salvation for men. The Only begotten Son of God Jesus Christ.

Hebrews 3: 3 The Son is the radiance of God's glory and the exact representation of his being, sustaining all things by his powerful word. After he had provided purification for sins, he sat down at the right hand of the Majesty in heaven. 4 So he became as much superior to the angels as the name he has inherited is superior to theirs.

Hebrews 2:17 For this reason he had to be made like them, fully human in every way, in order that he might become a merciful and faithful high priest in service to God, and that he might make atonement for the sins of the people.

Galatians 4:1 I mean that the heir, as long as he is a child, is no different from a slave, though he is the owner of everything, 2 but he is under guardians and managers until the date set by his father. 3 In the same way we also, when we were children, were enslaved to the elementary principles of the world. 4 But when the fullness of time had come, God sent forth his Son, born of woman, born under the law, 5 to redeem those who were under the law, so that we might receive adoption as sons.

Desiring God.org writes Why is Jesus called "Son of Man"? Let me give a common understanding and then a more sophisticated historical understanding.
The common understanding is that "Son of God" implies his deity—which it does—and that "Son of Man" implies his humanity, which it does too.
He was a son of man, that is, a human being. And he is the Son of God, in that he has always existed as the Eternally Begotten One who comes forth from the Father forever. He always has, and he always will. He is the Second Person of the Trinity with all of the divine nature fully in him.
He is born of a virgin. He had a human father, but he did not have sex with this virgin until Jesus was conceived. He

was conceived of the Holy Spirit in the virgin Mary. Thus, he is human—fully human. The Bible wants to emphasize that he is fully human.
So that is the common understanding: he is both divine and he is human—two natures, one person.

As Jesus, the Son of God, gave up the Spirit and died for our sins, he becomes known as the sacrificial lamb or Passover lamb that was given up for us. Here he is seen as the lamb of God who takes away the sins of the world and who is to come again in glory.

Jesus is the Lamb of God who was spotless and blameless. He was without sin and is perfect. He was sent on our behalf for the redemption, salvation, and forgiveness of sins. By his body and blood represented as the Passover lamb of the offering of bread and wine. Jesus, the Son of God, is exalted to the highest position and given a throne as the lamb of God. Who is worthy and receives praise honor and glory.

1 Peter 1:19 *It was the precious blood of Christ, the sinless, spotless Lamb of God. 20 He was chosen before the creation of the world, but was revealed in these last times for your sake. 21 Through him you believe in God, who raised him from the dead and glorified him, and so your faith and hope are in God.*

Colossians 1:22 *But now he has reconciled you by Christ's physical body through death to present you holy in his sight, without blemish and free from accusation--*

Philippians 2:6 Who, being in very nature God, did not consider equality with God something to be used to his own advantage; 7 rather, he made himself nothing by taking the very nature of a servant, being made in human likeness. 8 And being found in appearance as a man, he humbled himself by becoming obedient to death-- even death on a cross! 9 Therefore God exalted him to the highest place and gave him the name that is above every name, 10 that at the name of Jesus every knee should bow, in heaven and on earth and under the earth, 11 and every tongue acknowledge that Jesus Christ is Lord, to the glory of God the Father.

Revelations 5:4 I wept and wept because no one was found who was worthy to open the scroll or look inside. 5 Then one of the elders said to me, "Do not weep! See, the Lion of the tribe of Judah, the Root of David, has triumphed. He is able to open the scroll and its seven seals." 6 Then I saw a Lamb, looking as if it had been slain, standing at the center of the throne, encircled by the four living creatures and the elders. The Lamb had seven horns and seven eyes, which are the seven spirits of God sent out into all the earth. 7 He went and took the scroll from the right hand of him who sat on the throne.

Revelations 5:12 In a loud voice they were saying: "Worthy is the Lamb, who was slain, to receive power and wealth and wisdom and strength and honor and glory and praise!" 13 Then I heard every creature in heaven and on earth and under the earth and on the sea, and all that is in them, saying: "To him who sits on the throne and to the Lamb be praise and honor and glory and power, for ever and ever!"

Revelations 22:3 No longer will there be any curse. The throne of God and of the Lamb will be in the city, and his servants will serve him.

There are three phases of the existence of Jesus. As he was in heaven as he came down from heaven and as he ascended back into heaven.

In the beginning Jesus is the Word of God who was in the beginning with God who spoke all things into existence.

Jesus is The Son of God who came down from heaven and was born a man.

Jesus is the lamb of God who gave up his body and blood and ascended back into heaven and is seated at the right hand of God.

This is Jesus Christ who was the Word of God, who is the Son of God, and who is the Lamb of God who is to come again. Who was who is and who is to come.

Holy is the Lord Jesus Christ the Son of God who has been given all power and authority. The Word of God who was in the beginning with God. The Son of God who is the only begotten of the Father. The Lamb of God who died for our sins and who is to come again.

In conclusion, Holy is the Lord Jesus Christ the Son of God who has been given all power and authority. The

Word of God who was in the beginning with God. The Son of God who is the only begotten of the Father. The Lamb of God who died for our sins and who is to come again in his Glory.

The Word of God who spoke all things into existence. The Word of God who came down from heaven and was born a man.

The Son of God who was born of a virgin and born of God. The Son of God who came into the world, but the world did not recognize him although he created the world.

The Son of God who gave up his body and blood for us.

The Lamb of God who was the Passover lamb given up for us for salvation. The Lamb of God who takes away the sins of the world and who is to come again. Who was, who is, and who is to come, the Almighty.

Chapter 7: The Good Shepherd

Christ is the Good Shepherd, and we are His sheep. He leads those who are His to rivers of everlasting life.

A Shepherd or sheep herder is someone who leads the flock, guides the flock, shows them the way, watches over and protects the flock. A Shepherd loves his sheep tends to his sheep and feeds them.

Christ is the Good Shepherd, and he leads us and guides us in the truth, He is the way and shows us the way, He watches over us and protects us. He loves us and feeds us with the truth.

As sheep we follow the Shepherd, and we trust in Him. Christ says to his sheep, follow me I am the way the truth and the life. We follow in the ways of Christ which is the ways of God.

We listen to his voice and we follow His word. Christ says that he knows his sheep and his sheep know him.

He says if one sheep out of hundred was to go astray and wander off he would leave the 99 to retrieve the one who is lost.

When we follow him, we are close to the flock and the Shepherd but if we wander off, we can become lost, but He loves us and will guide us back to Him.

He is the Good Shepherd that leads his sheep to everlasting life. His sheep follow him and in his ways for he is the way to the truth and life.

We follow in his example and what he taught through his word. That his sheep trust in him and follow him and we walk in his ways.

He tells us that his ways are righteousness and those follow the light delight in what is good and faithful.

The Good Shepherd knows his sheep and will separate his sheep from the goats. The sheep are the faithful and fruitful ones of Christ, believers in Christ and the goats are the unbelievers who work the fruitless deeds of darkness.

Those who are in Christ are His sheep and He is their Shepherd. He is over the flock and He leads them to light and salvation. He shows them the way and gives them eternal life.

That no man can snatch them out his hand. He leads them to green pastures and rivers everlasting in which they inherit the earth and everlasting life.

Christ is the Good Shepherd, and we are His sheep. He leads those who are His to rivers of everlasting life.

John 10:11 "I am the good shepherd. The good shepherd lays down his life for the sheep.

John 10:14 "I am the good shepherd; I know my sheep and my sheep know me—

John 10:25 Jesus answered, "I did tell you, but you do not believe. The works I do in my Father's name testify about me, 26 but you do not believe because you are not my sheep.

John 10:27 My sheep listen to my voice; I know them, and they follow me.

John 10:28 I give them eternal life, and they shall never perish; no one will snatch them out of my hand.

A Shepherd or sheep herder is someone who leads the flock, guides the flock, shows them the way, watches over and protects the flock. A Shepherd loves his sheep tends to his sheep and feeds them. Christ is the Good Shepherd, and he leads us and guides us in the truth, He is the way and shows us the way, He watches over us and protects us. He loves us and feeds us with the truth.

John 10:1 "Very truly I tell you Pharisees, anyone who does not enter the sheep pen by the gate, but climbs in by some other way, is a thief and a robber.

2 The one who enters by the gate is the shepherd of the sheep.

3 The gatekeeper opens the gate for him, and the sheep listen to his voice. He calls his own sheep by name and leads them out.

4 When he has brought out all his own, he goes on ahead of them, and his sheep follow him because they know his voice.

5 But they will never follow a stranger; in fact, they will run away from him because they do not recognize a stranger's voice

John 14:6 Jesus answered, "I am the way and the truth and the life. No one comes to the Father except through me.

John 11:25 Jesus said to her, "I am the resurrection and the life. The one who believes in me will live, even though they die;

As sheep we follow the Shepherd, and we trust in Him. Christ says to his sheep, follow me I am the way the truth and the life. We follow in the ways of Christ which is the ways of God. We listen to his voice and we follow His word.

John 12:26 Whoever serves me must follow me; and where I am, my servant also will be. My Father will honor the one who serves me.

Matthew 4:19 "Come, follow Me," Jesus said, "and I will make you fishers of men."

Christ says that he knows his sheep and his sheep know him. He says if one sheep out of hundred was to go astray and wander off he would leave the 99 to retrieve the one who is lost. When we follow him, we are close to the flock and the Shepherd but if we wander off, we can become lost, but He loves us and will guide us back to Him.

Ezekiel 34:31 31 You are my sheep, the sheep of my pasture, and I am your God, declares the Sovereign LORD.'

Luke 15:3 Then Jesus told them this parable:

4 "Suppose one of you has a hundred sheep and loses one of them. Doesn't he leave the ninety-nine in the open country and go after the lost sheep until he finds it? 5 And when he finds it, he joyfully puts it on his shoulders 6 and goes home. Then he calls his friends and neighbors together and says, 'Rejoice with me; I have found my lost sheep.'

Luke 15:7 In the same way, there is more joy in heaven over one lost sinner who repents and returns to God than over ninety-nine others who are righteous and have not strayed away!

He is the Good Shepherd that leads his sheep to everlasting life. His sheep follow him and in his ways for he is the way to the truth and life. We follow in his example and what he taught through his word. That his sheep trust in him and follow him and we walk in his ways. He tells us that his ways are righteousness and those follow the light delight in what is good and faithful.

Psalms 23:1 The LORD is my shepherd; I shall not want. 2 He makes me lie down in green pastures, he leads me beside quiet waters, 3 he refreshes my soul. He guides me along the paths of righteousness for his name's sake.

Psalm 145:17 The LORD is righteous in all his ways and faithful in all he does.

Psalm 18:30 As for God, his way is perfect: The LORD's word is flawless; he shields all who take refuge in him.

Deuteronomy 32:4 He is the Rock, his works are perfect, and all his ways are just. A faithful God who does no wrong, upright, and just is he.

Psalm 119:68 You are good and do good; teach me your statutes.

Psalms 37:3-5 Trust in the LORD, and do good; Dwell in the land, and feed on His faithfulness. Delight yourself also in the LORD, And He shall give you the desires of your heart. Commit your way to the LORD, Trust also in Him, And He shall bring it to pass.

Psalms 23:4 Even though I walk through the darkest valley, I will fear no evil, for you are with me; your rod and your staff, they comfort me.

A Shepherd carries a rod or staff, and He leads the sheep to green pastures and water everlasting. He refreshes the soul by salvation and guides us in truth and righteousness.

Matthew 5:6 Blessed are those who hunger and thirst for righteousness, for they will be filled.

The Good Shepherd knows his sheep and will separate his sheep from the goats. The sheep are the faithful and fruitful ones of Christ, believers in Christ and the goats are the unbelievers who work the fruitless deeds of darkness. Those who are in Christ are His sheep and He is their Shepherd.

Matthew 25:31 "When the Son of Man comes in his glory, and all the angels with him, he will sit on his glorious throne. 32 All the nations will be gathered before him, and he will separate the people one from another as a shepherd separates the sheep from the goats. 33 He will put the sheep on his right and the goats on his left. 34 "Then the King will say to those on his right, 'Come, you who are blessed by my Father; take your inheritance, the kingdom prepared for you since the creation of the world.

He is over the flock and He leads them to light and salvation. He shows them the way and gives them eternal life. That no man can snatch them out his hand. He leads them to green pastures and rivers everlasting in which they inherit the earth and everlasting life.

John 21:17 He *said to him the third time, "Simon, son of John, do you love Me?" Peter was grieved because He said to him the third time, "Do you love Me?" And he said to Him, "Lord, You know all things; You know that I love You." Jesus *said to him, "Tend My sheep.

Matthew 5:5 Blessed are the meek, for they will inherit the earth.

———————————

Tell the Lord thank you .com writes, John 10:27 - My sheep hear My voice, and I know them, and they follow Me.

A shepherd in ancient times did not have thousands of sheep to look after. He had a small flock, and he knew each one of them.

In this text, Jesus says He is the "Shepherd" of the "sheep" and we Christians are "sheep" who belong to Jesus and are known by Jesus.

Because we are the "Shepherd" sheep and we belong to Him and he knows us, we know His voice and we respond to His commands because His voice we have heard and His voice we recognize.

What is it that makes us able to recognize anyone's voice or cause their voice to get stuck in our memory bank? I am not sure, but it just goes to show us the mystery of God's amazing and detailed work He put into His creation of human beings.

One thing that is amazing about the "Shepherd" and their "sheep" is the relationship that forms between them as they daily spend time together in fellowship, prayer, and study of His Word.

The "Shepherd" watches out for His "sheep". He provides for them. He treats our injuries and heals all our disease. He guides us away from danger, even when we (sheep) seem to be intent on getting into danger by trying to go our own way at times.

As "sheep", we depend on the "Shepherd" and we gladly follow Him because he is our protector. He can be trusted, and we can rely completely on Him to do just what He says.

The "Shepherd knows His "sheep", He loves us, cares for us and He knows our name. He lives in us by way of His Holy Spirit, He walks with us wherever we go, He feeds us the Bread of Heaven through His Word, He guides us, He is a *lamp unto our feet and the light that directs our path, and He protects us from hurt, harm and danger.*

Each and every day we hear a lot of voices and at times they can be overwhelming.

How do we discern what voice to listen to, which voice to follow?

There are a lot of voices out there telling you who you are, where you should go, what you should want, who you should be, what you should do, go here, go there, do this, do that, buy this, believe this, believe that, buy that, drive this, drive that, live here, live there and on and on with one voice after another being heard.

Whose voice are you listening to? Whose "truth" are you being convinced by? Who are you following?

Just as a baby knows his or her mother's voice and follows them around when they hear it, Jesus declares on today that His "sheep" knows His voice and follow Him and no other.

How do we hear God's voice? We hear Him in His Word that is found in the bible. That is where we can be sure that it is God that is speaking to us and it is Him who reveals Himself to us in His command for us to "follow Him".

As "sheep" of the "Good Shepherd" we as Christians need to extend the same love and care to those outside the church walls, the aged, needy, widow, poor, needy, sick, and lost.

Jesus is the "Good Shepherd" that laid down His life the sheep over 2k years ago on a hill called "Calvary". Why aren't you following Him?

Perhaps you are not His "sheep" because you have not accepted Him as the Savior of your soul, but instead rejected Him. If you are willing to repent of your sins, confess Jesus as Lord and believe in your heart that God raised Him from the dead, you too can become one of the "sheep" that hears the "Shepherd" voice and follow Him. Jesus is the Shepherd of his "sheep". He calls them, and they follow. He gives them life. He protects them. Verse 28 says "I give them eternal life, and they will never perish. No one will snatch them out of my hand."

Do you stand in need of the "Shepherd" leading on today?

He is able to lead, guide and direct you if you are willing to humbly come to Him. As a Matter of fact, He bids us to come to Him on today so that we may find the help we need in our time of trouble.

The "sheep" hears the "Shepherd voice and follows His call of obedience and joy.

The "sheep" hears the "Shepherd" voice and follows Him. Do you hear His voice? Do you recognize His voice? Will you follow His voice?

Psalm 23:2 "He maketh me to lie down in green pastures: he leadeth me beside the still waters."

This is a picture of complete peacefulness and rest. God's people, like sheep, do not have enough sense to go to the "pastures" for food or find the "still waters".

So, the Good Shepherd leads His beloved ones to a place of sustenance and rest (65:11-13; Ezek. 34:14; Rev. 7:17).

The good Shepherd knows the needs of His sheep, and He leads them to the food (green pastures), where they can find this food. For the believer, this food is the Word of God. We are told to eat of this Word.

Luke 4:4 "And Jesus answered him, saying, It is written, That man shall not live by bread alone, but by every word of God."

Jeremiah 15:16 "Thy words were found, and I did eat them; and thy word was unto me the joy and rejoicing of mine heart: for I am called by thy name, O LORD God of hosts."

We know then, we are to eat the Word. Now let us look at this still water. Let us look at this water in the next few Scriptures. Notice one statement above about the water, before we begin. This water is not forced upon the sheep. They are led to the water, and they may or not partake of that water. It is available, but they must drink.

John 4:14 "But whosoever drinketh of the water that I shall give him shall never thirst; but the water that I shall give him shall be in him a well of water springing up into everlasting life."

This water of the Good Shepherd seems to have life everlasting in it. John 7:38 "He that believeth on me, as the scripture hath said, out of his belly shall flow rivers of living water."

This living water then is the Spirit. It is available to all believers. Notice now, that the Great Shepherd has provided the Word to eat and the Spirit to drink in. It is the sheep's option whether to take it or not.

1 Corinthians 12:13 "For by one Spirit are we all baptized into one body, whether [we be] Jews or Gentiles, whether [we be] bond or free; and have been all made to drink into one Spirit."

In conclusion, the Good Shepherd leads his sheep to green pastures and waters everlasting. The Good Shepherd cares for his sheep and lays down his life for his sheep. The sheep hear his voice and follow the Shepherd.

Christ is the Good Shepherd who leads us out of darkness and into the light. He leads us to salvation and eternal life. He is the way and through him he leads us to the Father.

There is no way to heaven but through Christ, he is the way, the truth, and life. He is the way that leads to truth and eternal life.

The Good Shepherd knows his sheep by name, and he feeds his sheep. Christ knows us and teaches us through life and his word and truth.

Even if one were to go astray Christ would go and retrieve that one. He watches over us and in him we are safe.

He leads us to green pastures which is heaven on earth and to rivers everlasting which is eternal life.

He is the Good Shepherd and those who believe in him are his sheep. We follow the Good Shepherd, and we listen to his word.

Chapter 8: Light of the world

In the Book of Genesis, on the first day light was created. It was the light of the world. Christ is also the light of the world which came down from heaven.

He was the first begotten and before all creation just like light was the first creation and before all other creation.

Light gives life and sustains all creation just as Christ gives life and sustains all creation.

Light was separated from the darkness and God saw that the light was good. What is light? Light is the absence of darkness. There is no darkness in complete light. Light prevails over darkness and overcomes it.

Christ came into the world as a light to mankind. He is the true light who is absent of sin and righteous and there is no darkness in him.

He prevails over the power of darkness and leads those in darkness into the light. Which the darkness is sin and wickedness.

As we can see Christ is the light of the world that was first begotten before all creation. He is the light that came down from heaven to give light and life to mankind.

In the end we also see the lamb as the light of the world who gives his light forever.

Genesis 1: 1 In the beginning God created the heavens and the earth. 2 Now the earth was formless and empty, darkness was over the surface of the deep, and the Spirit of God was hovering over the waters. 3 And God said, "Let there be light," and there was light. 4 God saw that the light was good, and he separated the light from the darkness.

John 1:9 The one who is the true light, who gives light to everyone, was coming into the world.

10 He was in the world, and though the world was made through him, the world did not recognize him.

John 12:46 I have come into the world as a light, so that no one who believes in me should stay in darkness.

John 1:4 In him was life, and that life was the light of all mankind.

John 1:5 The light shines in the darkness, and the darkness has not overcome it.

John 3:19 This is the verdict: Light has come into the world, but people loved darkness instead of light because their deeds were evil. 20 Everyone who does evil hates the light and will not come into the light for fear that their deeds will be exposed. 21 But whoever lives by the truth comes into the light, so that it may be seen plainly that what they have done has been done in the sight of God.

John 8:12 When Jesus spoke again to the people, he said, "I am the light of the world. Whoever follows me will never walk in darkness but will have the light of life."

Colossians 1:12 and giving joyful thanks to the Father, who has qualified you to share in the inheritance of his holy people in the kingdom of light. 13 For he has rescued us from the dominion of darkness and brought us into the kingdom of the Son he loves,

1 John 1:5 This is the message we have heard from him and declare to you: God is light; in him there is no darkness at all.

Revelations 22:3 No longer will there be a curse upon anything. For the throne of God and of the Lamb will be there, and his servants will worship him. 4 They will see his face, and his name will be on their foreheads. 5 There will be no more night. They will not need the light of a lamp or the light of the sun, for the Lord God will give them light. And they will reign for ever and ever.

———————————

The light of the world in Genesis is talking about the creation of physical light. It is on the first day that light was created, and it was the first of all creation. This is also giving reference to Christ who is the light of the world and the first born of all creation.

In the same way light was created first and before all other creation, Christ is first begotten of the Father and before all creation. Just as light was brought into the world to overcome darkness, Christ is the light that is brought into the world to overcome evil.

On the first day God created light through His Word who spoke and manifested light into the world. God saw that this light was good. This is speaking of physical light which also gives reference to Christ being the spiritual light.

What is light? It is the absence of darkness. Light is also referred to as righteousness. What is righteous? It is the absence of wickedness. Light exposes the darkness and overcomes the darkness, just as light exposes wicked deeds and overcomes evil. Christ is the light and there is no darkness in him and that he is true light which He is righteousness and there is no sin in him. It is understood the world was in darkness and sin, and God sent his Son as light to the world and salvation. Not only did he bring light into world but also life for through him is eternal life. For light is life and Christ is that light that brings life. That Christ is the light that leads us out of darkness and saves us from sin. For there is no sin in him and he is righteous and true. Darkness is also referred to as evil wickedness and sin and death. Christ, who is the light, overcomes sin and death and brings us who are in sin and the darkness into his wonderful light.

Just as the sun gives life and is a sustaining power of creation. The Son, who is the light, gives life and is the sustaining power of creation. The Son also is the light that reveals God to all men. For once we were blind but now, we see. Once we were in darkness not knowing God, but Christ is the light that makes God known to men. The light also exposes our evil deeds and reveals that we are sinners understanding that we are in need of a savior.

Got questions writes I am the Light of the world" (John 8:12) is the second of seven "I AM" declarations of Jesus, recorded only in John's gospel, that point to His unique divine identity and purpose. In declaring Himself to be the Light of the world, Jesus was claiming that He is the exclusive source of spiritual light. No other source of spiritual truth is available to mankind.

There are two types of light in the world. We can perceive one, or both, or neither! When we are born into this world, we perceive physical light, and by it we learn of our Creator's handiwork in the things we see. However, although that light is good, there is another Light, a Light so important that the Son of God had to come in order to both declare and impart it to men. John 8:12 records, "When Jesus spoke again to the people, He said, 'I am the Light of the World. Whoever follows me will never walk in darkness but have the light of life.'" The allegory used by the Lord in this verse speaks of the light of His Truth, the light of His Word, the light of eternal Life. Those who perceive the true Light will never walk in spiritual darkness.

We take a candle into a room to dispel the darkness. Likewise, the Light of Jesus Christ has to be taken into the darkness of sin that engulfs the hearts and lives of those who are not following Him. That is the condition behind having this Light—that we follow Him. If we do not follow Him, we will not have this light, this truth, this eternal life.

Physical light is necessary for physical life. The earth would certainly change very rapidly if there were no longer any sunlight. A forest full of trees with very thick canopies of foliage high above has very little plant life on the ground except for moss or lichen, which needs little sunlight. Plants will never move away from the light—they are said to be positively phototropic, drawn to the light. In the same way, spiritual light is necessary for spiritual life, and this can be a good test of our standing in Christ. The believer will always tend toward spiritual things; he will always tend toward fellowship, prayer, the Word of God, and so on. The unbeliever always does the opposite (John 1:5; 3:19–20) because light exposes his evil, and he hates the light. Indeed, no man can come into the true spiritual light of Jesus Christ, unless he is enabled (John 6:37).

Following Jesus is the condition of two promises in John 8:12. First, His followers will never walk in darkness, which is a reference to the assurance of salvation we enjoy. As true followers of the Light, we will never follow the ways of sin, never live in a state of continually sinning (1 John 1:5–7). Rather, we repent of our sin in order to stay close to the Light of the world. The second promise is that we will reflect the Light of Life. Just as He came as the Light of the world, He commands us to be "lights," too. In Matthew 5:14–16 we see believers depicted as the light of the world. Just as the moon has no light of its own, reflecting the light of the sun, so are believers to reflect the Light of Christ so that all can see it in us. The Light is evident to others by the good deeds we do in faith and through the power of the Holy Spirit.

The emphasis here is maintaining a credible and obvious witness in the world, a witness that shows us to be faithful, God-honoring, trustworthy, sincere, earnest, and honest in all that we do. Also, we should always be ready to give an account of the hope that we have (1 Peter 3:15), for the gospel Light we have is not to be covered but made obvious for all to see and benefit from, that they, too, may leave the darkness and come into the Light.

Matthew 5:14-16 14 "You are the light of the world. A town built on a hill cannot be hidden. 15 Neither do people light a lamp and put it under a bowl. Instead, they put it on its stand, and it gives light to everyone in the house. 16 In the same way, let your light shine before others, that they may see your good deeds and glorify your Father in heaven.

Desiring God.org writes Light Triumphs over Darkness When John says in verse 5 that "the light shines in the darkness," he means that the Word has become flesh. Jesus has come into a dark world and is the light of the world. In John 8:12 Jesus says, "I am the light of the world." Right here in verse 9 it says, "The true light that enlightens every man was coming into the world. He was in the world, and the world was made through him, yet the world knew him not. He came to his own home, and his own people received him not." So, it is plain that Jesus is the one spoken of. He is the light in verse 5. He is the one who shines in the darkness.

The darkness is the world of evil and unbelief and death and judgment. John 3:19 says, "This is the judgment, that the light has come into the world, and men loved darkness rather than light because their deeds were evil." So, darkness is the power of evil and unbelief.

This Makes a Tremendous Difference

So, what verse 5 is saying is that Jesus Christ, the light of the world has entered into the darkness of evil and unbelief and lostness and death, and this darkness does not overcome Jesus. Now that makes a tremendous difference to those of us who believe in Jesus. In John 12:46 Jesus says, "I have come as light into the world that whoever believes in me may not remain in darkness." So, believers have passed from darkness to light. John 12:36 says, "While you have the light, believe in the light, that you may become sons of the light." When you believe in Jesus, not only do you leave the darkness and enter the light; you actually join the family of the light—you become children of the light. Paul said, "Once you were darkness, but now you are light in the Lord; walk as children of light" (Ephesians 5:8).

So, it makes a tremendous difference to us if the light triumphs, or the darkness overcomes it. And that is what verse 5 makes clear: "The light shines in the darkness, and the darkness has not overcome it." The light will triumph and that means Jesus will triumph and all those who believe in him, the children of the light, will triumph. We need to hear this today in America, because darkness is gaining ground on numerous fronts in our land.

Bible.Org writes Today's paint color is yellow since we will be talking about light. Would you agree that the sun is the biggest yellow object you know? Bright sunlight warms us up and helps us to see the world around us. At night, the sun is shining on the other side of the earth, so it is dark here. When it is dark, you might feel afraid or alone. You might feel confused because you cannot see where to go. You can stumble and fall without light to guide you.

Light helps us to see where we are going so, we can keep going in the right direction and not get lost. Think of how a light at the end of a dark hallway directs you to the doorway so you do not keep bumping into the walls. So, for this lesson the color yellow represents light and direction.

In our world, we depend on electricity to give us light in the dark. Just turn on a lamp or a switch and get instant light. When Jesus lived on the earth, there was no electricity. People depended on candles and oil lamps for light at night. Imagine what it would have been like to look out your window at night without any streetlights—anywhere! Consider how dark it could have been.

1. If you have been in a very dark place, what was that like?

2. How does darkness make you feel?

Jesus understood how much we need light to direct us in the darkness. One day He was attending a big festival in Jerusalem during the fall. A major part of that festival was the lighting of huge lamps that illuminated the entire temple area. Those were not the small oil lamps most people owned. They were really big ones that shone light all over the temple building. The people would gather together in that light to sing praises to God and dance. Right in the middle of that time of singing and dancing, Jesus told the crowd something about Himself.

3. Read John 8:12.
- What does Jesus call himself?
- What is the promise to those who follow Jesus?

You already thought about darkness and how it makes you feel. Sometimes scared, sometimes confused, and sometimes lonely. When there's darkness all around us, light gives us direction to follow the right path. Light gives us security and makes us feel less lonely. Light helps us to see clearly.

Suppose I turned on a flashlight and pointed it at various objects in a dark room while asking you "What do you see?" After looking at several objects and hearing your responses, I could ask, "How did you know what I wanted you to see?" You would probably answer that the light directed your eyes. The light helped you to see each object better. Light gives us direction.

4. What do you think Jesus meant when He said He was the light of the world? (Consider the flashlight example above.)

Darkness in the Bible usually means not knowing God and His love. But Jesus promises His light leads to life. Life in the Bible means spiritual life—knowing God and His wonderful love for us and living a life that pleases God. Light gives us direction. So, our yellow paint represents both light and direction.

Not too long after that festival of lights with the huge lamps, Jesus was in Jerusalem walking around. As Jesus went along, He saw a man who was born blind. That man had never seen the sun or the sky. You might know someone who is blind. Most of the time people who are blind cannot see any light at all. They are always in the dark.

―――――――――――

    In Conclusion, Jesus is the light of the world who came down from heaven as light and salvation.

Just as light was the first creation on the first day, Jesus is the first begotten of God and first born of all creation.

Light is representative of righteousness and goodness. It is also the light that exposes sin and the light that leads to salvation.

Jesus Christ is that light and in him he leads us out of darkness, death, and sin and brings us into his light, eternal life, and righteousness.

Christ is the light of the world that leads men out of darkness. He is the light of the world being the first begotten before all creation.

He is the first just as light was created on the first day. He is the light that came down from heaven and shines upon all men.

He is the light of truth and salvation. He came to shed light and reveal the truth to us about God and to be sent into the world as salvation for all people.

He is the light of truth and salvation that exposes men of their evil deeds and reveals that as sinners we are in need of salvation.

He is that light that saves us from sin and death and leads us out of the darkness. He lights up the way and shows us how to please the Father.

He reveals that God is light and there is no darkness in him. Therefore, God is Holy and there is no evil in him.

Christ is light from true light because he is from God and he is Holy and there is no sin in him.

He is the light that exposes the darkness and overcomes evil. Christ is the light that exposes sin and overcomes death. He is the light of the world that defeats sin and death and overcomes the darkness of this world.

Just as the sun overcomes darkness each new morning Christ is the light that overcomes evil and gives us new life and makes us a new creation in him. He is the light of the world and through him we let our light shine in the world.

I would like to quote 1 John 1:5-10 *"Jesus told us God is light and doesn't have any darkness in him. Now we are telling you. If we say we share in life with God and keep on living in the dark, we are lying and not living by the truth. But if we live in the light, as God does, we share in life with each other. And the blood of his Son Jesus washes all our sins away. If we say we have not sinned, we are fooling ourselves, and the truth is not in our hearts. But if we confess our sins to God, he can forgive us and take our sins away. If we say we have not sinned, we make God a liar, and his message is not in our hearts.*

Chapter 9: Victory in Christ

In Genesis it mentions the very first prophecy where God declares that His Son will crush the head of the serpent. That Christ has victory over Satan and evil. That he has victory over death and sin. He is our victory, and we have victory in Christ.

In revelations it speaks of when Christ returns and how he will destroy his enemies with breath. That he returns with the armies of angels and defeats his enemies. The last enemy to be destroyed is death.

In Christ we have eternal life and salvation. He defeated death and sin and through him we have eternal life and salvation. We have victory over death and victory over sin in Christ.

The Bible says that all his enemies will be made a footstool, and all will confess He is lord. God defeats evil and redeems the world through his Son.

By the death of his Son sin is destroyed and the penalty of sin and death is destroyed by his death and resurrection which gives us victory over death and sin through Christ.

In the book of Genesis, it foretells of the first prophecy given by God where He declares that the seed of the woman will be at enmity with the seed of the serpent.

That the serpent would strike his heel and the He would crush the head of the serpent.

The seed of the woman is Jesus Christ, and the seed of the serpent is the Devil.

The serpent will strike his heel means it will be a temporary wound but the crushing of the head of the serpent is a permanent fatal destruction.

This prophecy is revealing how Christ suffers a temporary wound by dying for our sins but how He is resurrected and defeats death and sin and ultimately destroying all evil and the Devil.

He has victory over the Devil and crushes the head of the serpent. He defeats and destroys death and sin and is victorious over the grave and sin and through him we have the resurrection and eternal life.

We have victory in Christ for he has triumphed over all evil. He has brought us out of the kingdom of darkness and into his kingdom of light.

_____

In the book of Genesis, it foretells of the first prophecy given by God where He declares that the seed of the woman will be at enmity with the seed of the serpent.

Genesis 3:13 Then the LORD God said to the woman, "What is this you have done?" The woman said, "The serpent deceived me, and I ate."

3:14 So the LORD God said to the serpent, "Because you have done this, "Cursed are you above all livestock and all wild animals! You will crawl on your belly and you will eat dust all the days of your life.

3:15 And I will put enmity between you and the woman, and between your offspring and hers; he will crush your head, and you will strike his heel."

The seed of the woman is Jesus Christ, and the seed of the serpent is the Devil.

Galatians 4:4 But when the fullness of the time came, God sent forth His Son, born of a woman, born under the Law,

Isaiah 7:14 Therefore the Lord Himself will give you a sign: Behold, a virgin will be with child and bear a son, and she will call His name Immanuel.

Luke 1:31 And behold, you will conceive in your womb and bear a son, and you shall name Him Jesus.

Galatians 3:16 Now the promises were spoken to Abraham and to his seed. He does not say, "And to seeds," as referring to many, but rather to one, "And to your seed," that is, Christ.

The Promise to Abraham is the seed of Christ and the children of light. The seed of the serpent is the children of darkness and the serpent is the devil.

Ephesians 5:8 for at one time you were darkness, but now you are light in the Lord. Walk as children of light.

1 Thessalonians 5:5 You are all children of the light and children of the day. We do not belong to the night or to the darkness.

Ephesians 5:11 Have nothing to do with the fruitless deeds of darkness, but rather expose them.

John 3:19 This is the verdict: Light has come into the world, but people loved darkness instead of light because their deeds were evil.

1 John 3:10 By this it is evident who are the children of God, and who are the children of the devil: whoever does not practice righteousness is not of God, nor is the one who does not love his brother.

John 8:44 For you are the children of your father the devil, and you love to do the evil things he does. He was a murderer from the beginning. He has always hated the truth because there is no truth in him. When he lies, it is consistent with his character; for he is a liar and the father of lies.

The serpent will strike his heel means it will be a temporary wound but the crushing of the head of the serpent is a permanent fatal destruction.

It is through Christ we have victory over sin and death, and he brings us out of darkness into the light. He exposes our evil deeds and shows us we are in need of salvation. It is through his death that we are saved. Not only from death but from sin. His death and resurrection give us victory over death and by his light we have victory over sin. That through Christ we have victory over the devil and evil and our brought into his Kingdom of light and righteousness.

He destroys death and the grave when he died on the cross and resurrected to life. When he returns and resurrects the dead the saying will be true "oh death where is your sting" for he has defeated death and the grave and overcame sin. He is victorious over sin and death and he ultimately is victorious over the devil when he is cast in the lake of fire. By his stripes we are healed and by his death we are saved. We are victorious because He is victorious, and Christ is our Victory.

1 Corinthians 15:54 When the perishable has been clothed with the imperishable, and the mortal with immortality, then the saying that is written will come true: "Death has been swallowed up in victory."

1 Corinthians 15:55 O death, where is thy sting? O grave, where is thy victory?

15:56 The sting of death is sin, and the power of sin is the law. 57 But thanks be to God! He gives us the victory through our Lord Jesus Christ.

John 12:36 Believe in the light while you have the light, so that you may become children of light."

1 Peter 2:24 "He himself bore our sins" in his body on the cross, so that we might die to sins and live for righteousness; "by his wounds you have been healed."

Colossians 1:12 and giving joyful thanks to the Father, who has qualified you to share in the inheritance of his holy people in the kingdom of light.

1:13 For he has rescued us from the dominion of darkness and brought us into the kingdom of the Son he loves, 14 in whom we have redemption, the forgiveness of sins.

When Christ returns as King, He will defeat His enemies and establish His righteous kingdom over all the earth. He will defeat evil and will cast the devil in the lake of fire.

Revelations 19:15 Coming out of his mouth is a sharp sword with which to strike down the nations. "He will rule them with an iron scepter." He treads the winepress of the fury of the wrath of God Almighty.

2 Thessalonians 2:8 And then the lawless one will be revealed, whom the Lord Jesus will overthrow with the breath of his mouth and destroy by the splendor of his coming.

Revelations 17:14 They will wage war against the Lamb, but the Lamb will triumph over them because he is Lord of lords and King of kings--and with him will be his called, chosen and faithful followers."

Revelations 20:10 and the devil who had deceived them was thrown into the lake of fire and sulfur where the beast and the false prophet were, and they will be tormented day and night forever and ever.

Got Questions.com writes as followers of Jesus Christ, we all want to live a triumphant Christian life. The Bible assures us that God and His Son Jesus are Victors and that believers can share in their victories: "But thanks be to God! He gives us the victory through our Lord Jesus Christ" (1 Corinthians 15:57). In a practical sense, how can we experience the victorious life that has been made possible in Christ? How can we achieve victory in Jesus?

Victory ultimately belongs to the Lord our God (1 Samuel 17:47). Since the days of Israel's Exodus from Egypt, whenever God's people depended on Him alone, He gave them victory over their enemies (Exodus 15). Old Testament prophets consistently pointed to a future Savior who would bring the fullest expression of God's triumph: "Rejoice greatly, Daughter Zion! Shout, Daughter Jerusalem! See, your king comes to you, righteous and victorious, lowly and riding on a donkey, on a colt, the foal of a donkey" (Zechariah 9:9; see also Psalm 110:1). We know these prophecies refer to Jesus Christ, the promised Messiah, who has overcome the world (John 16:33).

Jesus won the supreme victory at the cross. Sin was atoned for, and the power of sin and death was broken (see John 12:31 and 1 Peter 2:24). After Christ's crucifixion and burial, He rose from the dead three days later, and now we share that victory. Satan thought he had won the ultimate contest with the death of Christ. Instead, that death released our chains, set us free from the prison of sin, and disarmed the supernatural powers of evil: "When you were dead in your sins and in the uncircumcision of your flesh, God made you alive with Christ. He forgave us all our sins, having canceled the charge of our legal indebtedness, which stood against us and condemned us; he has taken it away, nailing it to the cross. And having disarmed the powers and authorities, he made a public spectacle of them, triumphing over them by the cross" (Colossians 2:13–15).

The key to achieve victory in Jesus is faith in Christ: "For everyone born of God overcomes the world. This is the victory that has overcome the world, even our faith. Who is it that overcomes the world? Only the one who believes that Jesus is the Son of God" (1 John 5:4–5; see also Romans 8:37). The first step to victory in Jesus is accepting Christ as Savior. We receive the Lord by grace through faith, and we live in His victory by grace through faith as well. Our salvation is a gift of God's grace, and our victory in Jesus is a gift of God's grace (Ephesians 2:4–8; Galatians 3:3).

What is the extent of Jesus Christ's victory that He imparts to us? The victory that Jesus shares with us includes victory over the lust of the flesh, the lust of the eyes, and the pride of life (1 John 2:16). Our Lord's triumph over temptation and sin (Hebrews 4:15; see also Matthew 4:1–11) has become our victory as well: "Those who belong to Christ Jesus have crucified the flesh with its passions and desires" (Galatians 5:24; see also Romans 5:20–21). The apostle John elaborates: "But you know that he appeared so that he might take away our sins. And in him is no sin. No one *who lives in him keeps on sinning. No one who continues to sin has either seen him or known him. Dear children, do not let anyone lead you astray. The one who does what is right is righteous, just as he is righteous. The one who does what is sinful is of the devil, because the devil has been sinning from the beginning. The reason the Son of God appeared was to destroy the devil's work" (1 John 3:5–8).*

Jesus has overcome Satan and the powers of evil (John 14:30; 16:11; Mark 1:23–27; Luke 4:33–36), and He shares that victory with us. Jesus says, "I saw Satan fall like lightning from heaven. I have given you authority to trample on snakes and scorpions and to overcome all the power of the enemy; nothing will harm you" (Luke 10:18–19; see also Ephesians 1:21–22). The writer of Hebrews explains that Jesus took on flesh and blood and shared in our humanity "so that by his death he might break the power of him who holds the power of death—that is, the devil—and free those who all their lives were held in slavery by their fear of death" (Hebrews 2:14–15). We need not fear death or the devil because we share in Jesus Christ's victory over them (Acts 2:24; Romans 6:9; 8:38–39; 2 Timothy 1:10; Revelation 1:18).

As long as we remain in this fallen world, we will still have struggles to overcome and battles to fight. At times we will fall and fail. But we continue to get back up, asking God to equip us with His grace and power to overcome (2 Corinthians 12:9). As believers, we fight our battles in the spiritual realm, on our knees: "For though we live in the world, we do not wage war as the world does. The weapons we fight with are not the weapons of the world.

On the contrary, they have divine power to demolish strongholds" (2 Corinthians 10:3–4). God has given us spiritual armor to protect us from the powers of darkness that wage war against us (Ephesians 6:10–20).

Victory in Jesus is real and attainable now because our Lord Jesus has defeated Satan and every evil power of the world. We achieve victory in Jesus by resting in Christ (Matthew 11:28) and trusting Him to triumph for us (Romans 5:17). While we remain on earth, the Lord reigns victorious through those who have been delivered from the kingdom of darkness and translated into His glorious kingdom of light (1 Peter 2:9). However, a day will come when the victories of Jesus will be fully realized and celebrated in the new heavens and earth: "He will swallow up death forever. The Sovereign LORD will wipe away the tears from all faces; he will remove his people's disgrace from all the earth. The LORD has spoken" (Isaiah 25:8).

Got Questions writes," in his first letter to the Corinthians, Paul emphasizes the future resurrection of believers from the dead. There were some who denied the reality of the future resurrection, and Paul defends the truth to the believers in Corinth who had been deceived by that false teaching. Paul explains that the resurrection of believers in Christ is assured because Jesus Christ Himself rose from the dead (1 Corinthians 15:13).

Paul then looks forward to the second coming of Christ, when He will return with the resurrected saints and at which time He will destroy "all dominion, authority and power. For he must reign until he has put all his enemies under his feet. The last enemy to be destroyed is death" (1 Corinthians 15:24–26).

The enemies of God that will be destroyed include Satan, who by his deceit and lies ruined Adam and Eve and all humanity after them. All human beings inherit the sin nature from Adam (Romans 5:12), and all must live in bondage to sin unless delivered by Christ from their sinful state. Satan destroyed the innocence of Adam and Eve when he tempted them to rebel against God. But Jesus, who has redeemed the elect, will have the final victory over Satan and his demons when they are destroyed forever (Revelation 20:1–10).

Another enemy to be destroyed is sin, which all human beings are guilty of committing. On the cross, Jesus saved His people from the punishment and the power of sin. Believers need no longer fear God's wrath against their sin because Jesus took the punishment sinners deserve. He also delivered believers from the power of sin, granting us the ability to resist sin through the power of the Holy Spirit who dwells within and whose power is greater than the power of sin. One day, sin will be completely destroyed, and believers will no longer live in the presence of sin. The apostle John describes the New Jerusalem, which will come down from heaven and be entirely free from sin: "Nothing impure will ever enter it, nor will anyone who does what is shameful or deceitful, but only those whose names are written in the Lamb's book of life" (Revelation 21:27).

First Corinthians 15:26 says that the last enemy to be destroyed is death. Death will be the last of all because it is the "wages of sin" (Romans 6:23) and must continue to exist until sin has come to an end. Death was the last of the enemies to come, and it will be the last to be destroyed. How will this happen? Those who are in Christ will be raised to eternal life in the presence of God and will die no more. Even unbelievers will live eternally in the lake of fire, and there will be no more physical death for them (Mark 9:48). Physical death is the last enemy to be destroyed, both for the righteous and the wicked.

The defeat of death by the God of life proves the doctrine of the resurrection of the dead. Death can only be destroyed by the resurrection of both the wicked and the righteous, who will die no more. If there is no resurrection, then death will still rule, and people will be subject to it. The fact that death will be destroyed assures us of the resurrection. "When the perishable has been clothed with the imperishable, and the mortal with immortality, then the saying that is written will come true: 'Death has been swallowed up in victory.'"

    In conclusion, we have victory in Christ for he has victory on the cross. Christ paid the price for sins which was death. He was resurrected from death and received eternal glory. He is victorious over death and sin and has power to remove them.

In him we have victory over death, through his death, and in him we are saved. For he took all the sins of the world on the cross and nailed it to the cross.

That through his death and resurrection we have victory over sin and death. That the grave and death no longer have their sting.

Christ has victory over the evil one, Satan, and crushes his dominion and evil plans. Christ is victorious and is crowned with glory. He crushes the head of the serpent and brings us out of the kingdom of darkness and into his kingdom of light.

In him is light and that light leads men to righteousness and salvation. He gives us victory and power over sin and wickedness and gives us victory and power over death through the resurrection and eternal life.

Christ rules with an iron scepter and his kingdom is righteousness. He is victorious and reigns as King forever. He is the victory of God and in Christ we have victory.

Copyright © 2020 Michael J Hnatowicz III

All rights reserved. No part of this publication may be reproduced, distributed, or transmitted in any form or by any means, including photocopying, recordings, or other electronic or mechanical methods, without the prior written consent of the publisher, except in the case of brief quotations embodied in critical reviews and certain other noncommercial uses permitted by copyright law. For permission requests, write to the publisher, addressed "Attentions: Permissions Coordinator," at the address below.

ISBN: 978-1-7376810-1-4 (Paperback)

ISBN: 978-1-7376810-3-8 (Electronic Book)

Any references to historical events, real people, or real places are used fictitiously. Names, characters, and places are products of the authors imagination.

Book Design by Michael J Hnatowicz III

First Printing Edition, 2022

Meek Music and Publishing LLC

300 Colonial Center Parkway STE 100N
Roswell GA 30076

www.ingramcontent.com/pod-product-compliance
Lightning Source LLC
Chambersburg PA
CBHW050304120526
44590CB00016B/2485